500 Phrases by Freud

500 must-read phrases by Freud, organized by theme

Deivede E. Ferreira

DEAR READERS,

I am pleased to introduce Deivede Eder Ferreira, a renowned psychoanalyst and writer whose literary work is a reference in psychoanalytic introspection.

Deivede is the author of the book "Unveiling the Soul: Psychoanalytic Introspection Poems", a poetic work that addresses psychological and emotional issues of human beings in a profound and sensitive way. In his poems, the author explores the complexity of the human mind and invites the reader to a deep reflection on themselves.

In addition, Deivede is the organizer of the literary work "500 Phrases by Freud That You Can't Miss Reading, Organized by Theme". In this book, the author selects the most significant quotes from Sigmund Freud and organizes them by relevant themes to psychoanalysis. The work is a valuable reference for those seeking to understand Freud's theory in a clear and comprehensive way.

With a background in psychoanalysis, Deivede is a renowned professional recognized in his field of work. His literary work is an invitation to reflection and introspection, and his commitment to the search for self-knowledge is evident on every page of his works.

Deivede Eder Ferreira is an author who stands out for the depth and sensitivity of his work, which combines psychoanalytic reflection and literature in a unique and inspiring approach. His books are a source of inspiration for those seeking to understand the human mind and its complexities, and his work is a valuable contribution to literature and psychoanalysis.

DEDICATION:

I dedicate this work to the late Frederico Toldo, a great mentor and friend who taught me the importance of following my dreams and encouraged me to seek knowledge and excellence in my academic training. His example of determination and generosity will always be an inspiration in my life.

I also dedicate this work to my dear friend Michel Rezende, who has always been present in my academic journey and supported me in moments of difficulty. His friendship and trust were fundamental to my development as a person and professional.

Finally, I dedicate this work to my dear teachers at ISTA and PUC Minas, who provided me with the opportunity to acquire knowledge and skills in the fields of philosophy and psychoanalysis. Their commitment and dedication to sharing their knowledge were essential to my professional development.

To all of you, my eternal gratitude and admiration.

TABLE OF CONTENTS:

INTRODUCTION:

Psychoanalysis is one of the most influential fields in psychology, and Sigmund Freud is recognized as one of the most important theorists of this approach. His ideas about the human mind, including concepts such as the unconscious, libido, and Oedipus complex, have had a significant impact on psychology, literature, and the arts.

In this context, "500 Phrases by Freud That You Can't Miss, Organized by Theme" presents a carefully selected collection of quotes from Freud's work, organized by themes relevant to psychoanalysis. The book aims to offer readers a concise and accessible view of Freud's theories, through his own words, allowing a deep dive into the author's ideas.

Each chapter addresses a specific theme, such as sexuality, dreams, the unconscious, neurosis, psychosis, narcissism, Oedipus complex, ego, superego and id, therapy, culture, and society. The quotes offer insights and reflections on these themes, allowing readers to understand Freud's theories in a clear and comprehensive manner.

"500 Phrases by Freud That You Can't Miss,

Organized by Theme" is a valuable tool for psychology students, therapists, and academics seeking to understand Freud's psychoanalytic theory and its impact on the field of psychology. The work presents a deep and thought-provoking perspective on psychoanalytic theory, offering a clear and accessible introduction to Freud's work through his own words, in a thematic and comprehensive organization.

When reading this book, it is important to keep in mind that isolated phrases from a work can lead to misconceptions if one does not consider the historical and socio-cultural context in which they were produced. Freud lived in a time when many of the ideas and concepts that we now consider unacceptable or outdated were widely accepted.

Therefore, it is crucial to take into account the theory and context in which the quotes were written before drawing any conclusions or forming opinions. The ideas and concepts expressed by Freud in his writings were influenced by the culture, science, and society of his time, and it is necessary to understand these factors to fully grasp the meaning of his words.

Moreover, it is worth remembering that Freud's works are often the subject of controversy and criticism. Although his theories were innovative and influential, many of them have been criticized for being overly deterministic, sexist, and Eurocentric.

Therefore, when reading "500 Phrases by Freud That You Can't Miss", it is important to have a critical and reflective approach, taking into account the historical and socio-cultural context in which the quotes were produced and considering the criticisms and debates surrounding Freud's theories.

CHAPTER 1: SEXUALITY

"Sexuality is the key to understanding the human being" (Freud, 1905).

"Sexuality is the source of our most powerful energy" (Freud, 1931).

"Sexuality is such a strong impulse that it can lead us to madness or greatness" (Freud, 1931).

"Sexuality is a source of mystery and enigma, always challenging us to understand it" (Freud, 1905).

"Sexuality is one of the great themes of human life, always present in our experiences and desires" (Freud, 1905).

"Sexuality is a vital part of our nature, and repression of this energy can have serious consequences" (Freud, 1905).

"Sexuality is a profound and meaningful expression of our identity" (Freud, 1905).

"Sexuality is the root of our deepest emotional and psychological conflicts and problems" (Freud, 1905).

"Sexuality is a path to self-awareness and self-knowledge" (Freud, 1905).

"Sexuality is a crucial aspect of our emotional and psychological development" (Freud, 1905).

"Sexuality is a powerful force that can transform, liberate or destroy us" (Freud, 1931).

"Sexuality is a natural impulse that should be accepted and understood, not repressed or denied" (Freud, 1905).

"Sexuality is a source of pleasure, but also of pain and suffering" (Freud, 1905).

"Sexuality is a taboo topic in our culture, but we cannot ignore it if we want to understand ourselves and others" (Freud, 1905).

"Sexuality can lead us to deep emotional and intellectual discoveries, but it can also lead us to dead ends" (Freud, 1931).

"Sexuality is a matter of balance between the impulses of the ego and the id" (Freud, 1920).

"Sexuality is a form of interpersonal communication, but also a form of self-expression" (Freud, 1905).

"Sexuality is a fundamental part of our personality and can affect all areas of our life" (Freud, 1905).

"Sexuality is a complex and multifaceted topic that involves our emotions, desires, fears and fantasies" (Freud, 1905).

"Sexuality is a topic that will always be present in our lives, but we must learn to deal with it in a healthy and constructive way" (Freud, 1905).

"Sexuality is a fundamental aspect of our animal

nature, but it is also an expression of our humanity" (Freud, 1931).

"Sexuality is a subject that challenges us to explore the deepest mysteries of our existence" (Freud, 1905).

"Sexuality is a driving force that impels us to seek pleasure, but it can also lead us down dangerous and self-destructive paths" (Freud, 1931).

"Sexuality is an impulse that can be channeled in various ways, and it is important to find healthy ways to express it" (Freud, 1905).

"Sexuality is a source of fascination and horror, always surprising us with its strangest and most unexpected manifestations" (Freud, 1905).

"Sexuality is one of the great forces that shape our personality and make us who we are" (Freud, 1931).

"Sexuality is an expression of our deepest emotions, but it can also be a form of escapism and evasion from reality" (Freud, 1905).

"Sexuality is an integral part of our lives, and it is important to learn to deal with it consciously and responsibly" (Freud, 1905).

"Sexuality is one of the great questions of humanity, and will always be present as a source of mystery and perplexity" (Freud, 1905).

"Sexuality is one of the most powerful forces of human beings, capable of changing our lives and our perceptions of the world" (Freud, 1931).

References:

Freud, S. (1905). Three Essays on the Theory of Sexuality. Standard Edition, 7, 123-246.

Freud, S. (1920). Beyond the Pleasure Principle. Standard Edition, 18, 1-64.

Freud, S. (1931). Civilization and its Discontents. Standard Edition, 21, 57-145.

CHAPTER 2: DREAMS

"Dreams are the royal road to the unconscious" (Freud, 1900).

"Dreams are a complex and multifaceted psychic phenomenon that requires careful and detailed analysis" (Freud, 1900).

"Dreams are a manifestation of our inner world, revealing our deepest desires, fears, and conflicts" (Freud, 1900).

"Dreams are a symbolic expression of our unconscious and can reveal valuable insights about our psychic life" (Freud, 1900).

"The interpretation of dreams is the royal road to knowledge of the unconscious" (Freud, 1900).

"Dreams are one of the ways in which our unconscious tries to communicate with us" (Freud, 1900).

"Dreams are a means of wish fulfillment that occurs in the unconscious and manifests in the dream content" (Freud, 1900).

"Dreams are a way to self-knowledge, allowing us to better understand our desires, emotions, and motivations" (Freud, 1900).

"Dreams are a means by which our

unconscious protects us from traumatic or painful experiences" (Freud, 1900).

"Dreams are a fertile field for the study of psychoanalysis, revealing the dynamics of psychic life in its multiple dimensions" (Freud, 1900).

"The interpretation of dreams requires a systematic and careful approach based on a deep understanding of psychic processes" (Freud, 1900).

"The interpretation of dreams is a task that requires skill and sensitivity, as well as an in-depth knowledge of psychoanalytic theory" (Freud, 1900).

"Dreams are one of the primary forms of expression of the unconscious, allowing us to explore its depths and mysteries" (Freud, 1900).

"Dreams are a way to deal with the most difficult and complex emotions and conflicts that are often repressed in conscious life" (Freud, 1900).

"Dreams are a window into the human mind, offering a glimpse of the complexity and depth of psychic life" (Freud, 1900).

"Dreams are a manifestation of our most intimate and personal self, reflecting our deepest aspirations, fears, and desires" (Freud, 1900).

"The interpretation of dreams is an art that requires patience, dedication, and skill, but can bring profound and transformative insights" (Freud, 1900).

"Dreams are a way to deal with the traumas

and tensions of life, offering a safe space for the expression of our emotions and desires" (Freud, 1900).

"The analysis of dreams is a collaborative process between the analyst and the patient, requiring trust and openness from both parties" (Freud, 1900).

"Dreams are a means of access to our unconscious world, where we can find solutions to seemingly insoluble problems" (Freud, 1900).

"The interpretation of dreams is a powerful tool for understanding the psychic life, revealing hidden and unconscious aspects of our mind." (Freud, 1900)

"Dreams are a source of creativity and imagination, allowing us to explore possibilities that don't exist in everyday life." (Freud, 1900)

"The interpretation of dreams is not an exact science, but an art that requires intuition, sensitivity, and empathy." (Freud, 1900)

"Dreams are a form of self-expression, allowing us to explore our emotions and desires without censorship or judgment." (Freud, 1900)

"Dreams are a means of communication between the conscious and unconscious parts of our mind, allowing us to integrate these parts and become more whole." (Freud, 1900)

"The analysis of dreams is a powerful tool for personal transformation and psychological growth." (Freud, 1900)

"Dreams can reveal hidden aspects of our personality and patterns of behavior, helping us to understand ourselves better and to change positively." (Freud, 1900)

"The interpretation of dreams can be a difficult and challenging process, but one that is worth it for the knowledge and self-knowledge it can bring." (Freud, 1900)

"Dreams are a means of tapping into our creativity and imagination, allowing us to create new meanings and possibilities in our lives." (Freud, 1900)

"The interpretation of dreams is a way to explore the mysteries of the human mind, revealing deep and unexpected aspects of our psychic life." (Freud, 1900)

References:

Freud, S. (1900). The Interpretation of Dreams. Publisher: Basic Books; 1st Edition (November 12, 2010).

CHAPTER 3: UNCONSCIOUS

"The unconscious is the obscure part of our personality that deeply influences our behavior." (Freud, 1915)

"The unconscious is a sea of emotions, desires, and impulses that often operate without our awareness." (Freud, 1915)

"The unconscious is the source of many internal and external conflicts that we face throughout life." (Freud, 1915)

"The unconscious can be revealed through the analysis of dreams, slips of the tongue, and neurotic symptoms." (Freud, 1915)

"The unconscious is a region of our mind that is inaccessible to our conscious perception but exerts a powerful influence on us." (Freud, 1915)

"The unconscious is a source of creativity and imagination that can be used to solve problems and make decisions." (Freud, 1915)

"The unconscious is the place where many of our fears, desires, and repressed traumas reside, which can emerge in a distorted way in our dreams and behaviors." (Freud, 1915)

"The unconscious is the key to understanding

psychopathology, as many of our mental disorders have their origin in this obscure part of our personality." (Freud, 1915)

"The unconscious is a mysterious and fascinating region of the human mind that still has much to be explored." (Freud, 1915)

"The unconscious is the great unknown of psychology, but it is fundamental to understanding human behavior." (Freud, 1915)

"The unconscious can be compared to an iceberg, whose largest part is submerged, and we can only see the tip that emerges on the surface." (Freud, 1915)

"The unconscious is a reservoir of emotions and desires that are repressed by consciousness but continue to exert influence on behavior." (Freud, 1915)

"The unconscious is the seat of sexual and aggressive impulses that are often suppressed by society but do not disappear completely." (Freud, 1915)

"The unconscious is a region of the mind that is beyond reason and logic but has its own internal logic." (Freud, 1915)

"The unconscious is where many of our internal conflicts reside, which can manifest in disguised ways in our dreams and behaviors." (Freud, 1915)

"The unconscious is a source of resistance to change,

as we often cling to behavioral patterns that are unconscious and difficult to change." (Freud, 1915)

"The unconscious is a place of conflict between individual desires and needs and the demands of society and culture." (Freud, 1915)

"The unconscious is the source of many of our fantasies and dreams, which allow us to explore desires and impulses that we cannot express in real life." (Freud, 1915)

"The unconscious can be compared to a file of our life experience, where we store information that we cannot consciously access but continue to influence our behavior." (Freud, 1915)

"The unconscious is a place of conflict between the ego, the superego, and the id, which represent different parts of our personality." (Freud, 1923)

"The unconscious is the source of many of our automatic emotional reactions, which can be triggered by unconscious stimuli." (Freud, 1915)

"The unconscious is the source of our creativity and innovation, as it allows us to access ideas and solutions that are not evident to our conscious perception." (Freud, 1923)

"The unconscious is a place of conflict between our impulses and the demands of the external world, which often present themselves as obstacles to the fulfillment of our desires." (Freud, 1923)

"The unconscious is a source of psychic energy,

which can be channeled towards the attainment of our goals and the overcoming of our limitations." (Freud, 1923)

"The unconscious is a place of mystery and fascination, which invites us to explore the deepest secrets of the human mind." (Freud, 1915)

"The unconscious is a place of conflict between love and hate, sexuality and aggression, which often express themselves in a conflicting way in our interpersonal relationships." (Freud, 1923)

"The unconscious is a source of healing and transformation, as it allows us to access repressed experiences and emotions that need to be worked through in order to achieve a fulfilling and satisfying life." (Freud, 1923)

"The unconscious is a place of resistance to change, as we are often stuck in unconscious patterns of behavior that are difficult to change." (Freud, 1915)

"The unconscious is the source of our subjectivity, which allows us to create our own narratives and meanings about life and ourselves." (Freud, 1923)

"The unconscious is a place of freedom and autonomy, which allows us to transcend the limitations of culture and society and create our own paths in life." (Freud, 1923)

References:

Freud, S. (1915). The unconscious. The standard edition of the complete psychological works of Sigmund Freud, volume XIV. Hogarth Press.

Freud, S. (1923). The ego and the id. The standard edition of the complete psychological works of Sigmund Freud, volume XIX. Hogarth Press.

CHAPTER 4: NEUROSIS

"Neurosis is a conflict between desire and defense." (Freud, 1894)

"Neurosis is an attempted adaptation that has failed." (Freud, 1926)

"Neurosis is a symptom of conflict between the demands of the individual and the requirements of culture." (Freud, 1914)

"Neurosis is an expression of psychological conflicts that arise when the individual is unable to cope with the challenges of life." (Freud, 1909)

"Neurosis is a form of psychological suffering that can be treated with the help of psychoanalysis." (Freud, 1894)

"Neurosis is a state in which the person is unable to deal with their own emotional conflicts." (Freud, 1909)

"Neurosis is an attempt to avoid emotional suffering, but ends up generating even more suffering." (Freud, 1909)

"Neurosis is a form of ego defense against psychological suffering." (Freud, 1894)

"Neurosis is a psychological condition in which the individual experiences physical or emotional symptoms that have no obvious physical cause." (Freud, 1894)

"Neurosis is an expression of unresolved emotional conflicts that affect the individual's behavior and well-being." (Freud, 1914)

"Neurosis is a mental illness that can be treated with psychoanalysis, which aims to bring unconscious emotional conflicts to consciousness." (Freud, 1894)

"Neurosis is a form of ego defense against threats to its psychological integrity." (Freud, 1909)

"Neurosis is a way of dealing with painful emotions that arise when the individual is confronted with the demands of life." (Freud, 1914)

"Neurosis is an excessive emotional reaction to a situation that does not justify such a reaction." (Freud, 1914)

"Neurosis is an attempt to maintain the emotional homeostasis of the individual, but can lead to rigidity and inflexibility." (Freud, 1914)

"Neurosis is a psychological condition that results from conflicts between the ego and the id." (Freud, 1923)

"Neurosis is a form of resistance to change, as the individual is stuck in behavioral patterns that no longer work." (Freud, 1926)

"Neurosis is an expression of emotional conflicts that arise when the individual is unable to cope with the demands of life." (Freud, 1894)

"Neurosis is a form of unsuccessful adaptation that can lead to psychological suffering." (Freud, 1923)

"Neurosis is a form of psychological suffering that can affect all aspects of the individual's life." (Freud, 1914)

"Neurosis is a condition in which the individual experiences a conflict between their unconscious desires and the demands of external reality." (Freud, 1914)

"Neurosis is an attempt to find a solution to emotional conflicts, but often leads to a deterioration of mental health." (Freud, 1894)

"Neurosis is a form of self-deception in which the individual avoids facing their emotional conflicts." (Freud, 1914)

"Neurosis is a deviation from normal behavior that can result in problems with relationships, work, and health." (Freud, 1914)

"Neurosis is a form of expression of unconscious desires that cannot be fulfilled in real life." (Freud, 1914)

"Neurosis is an expression of emotional conflicts that arise when the individual is unable to cope with the demands of culture and society." (Freud, 1914)

"Neurosis is a condition in which the individual experiences psychological symptoms that are caused by unconscious emotional conflicts." (Freud, 1894)

"Neurosis is an attempt to find a solution to emotional conflicts, but often leads to a vicious cycle of suffering." (Freud, 1914)

"Neurosis is a form of ego defense against threats to its psychological integrity, but can lead to rigidity and inflexibility." (Freud, 1909)

"Neurosis is a form of psychological suffering that can be overcome through psychoanalysis, which aims to bring unconscious emotional conflicts to consciousness." (Freud, 1894)

References:

Freud, S. (1894). "On the neuroses of defense." The Standard Edition of the Complete Psychological Works of Sigmund Freud, 3:43-61.

Freud, S. (1926). "The question of lay analysis." The Standard Edition of the Complete Psychological Works of Sigmund Freud, 20:177-258.

Freud, S. (1914). "On narcissism: an introduction." The Standard Edition of the Complete Psychological Works of Sigmund Freud, 14:67-102.

Freud, S. (1909). "Notes upon a case of obsessional neurosis (the 'Rat Man')." The Standard Edition of the Complete Psychological Works of Sigmund Freud, 10:151-318.

Freud, S. (1894). "On the psychotherapy of hysteria." The Standard Edition of the Complete Psychological

Works of Sigmund Freud, 2:305-322.

Freud, S. (1909). "Analysis of a phobia in a five-year-old boy (the 'Little Hans' case)." The Standard Edition of the Complete Psychological Works of Sigmund Freud, 10:3-149.

Freud, S. (1923). "The ego and the id." The Standard Edition of the Complete Psychological Works of Sigmund Freud, 19:3-66. Freud, S. (1923). "Two contributions to the theory of sex." The Standard Edition of the Complete Psychological Works of Sigmund Freud, 18:235-259.

CHAPTER 5: PSYCHOSIS

"Psychosis is a condition in which the individual loses the ability to distinguish between the self and the external world." (Freud, 1911)

"Psychosis is a form of ego defense that can lead to alienation from reality and a withdrawal from significant interpersonal relationships." (Freud, 1911)

"Psychosis can be seen as an attempt to deal with primitive anxieties and fears related to separation and loss." (Freud, 1911)

"Psychosis is an extreme form of ego defense that requires a complex and integrated therapeutic approach." (Freud, 1911)

"Psychosis can be seen as an attempt to deal with internal conflicts through the creation of a new reality." (Freud, 1911)

"Psychosis is a form of psychological suffering that requires a deep understanding of the individual and their life history." (Freud, 1911)

"Psychosis can be seen as an attempt to deal with conflicting demands of instinct and culture." (Freud, 1911)

"Psychosis is a form of ego defense that can lead to a

loss of contact with reality and disconnection from significant interpersonal relationships." (Freud, 1911)

"Psychosis can be seen as an attempt to deal with fears and anxieties related to vulnerability and dependence." (Freud, 1911)

"Psychosis is an extreme form of psychological suffering that requires a therapeutic approach centered on understanding and empathy for the individual." (Freud, 1911)

References:

Freud, S. (1911). Formulations on the Two Principles of Mental Functioning. The Standard Edition of the Complete Psychological Works of Sigmund Freud, 12: 131-143.

Freud, S. (1911). Psycho-Analytic Notes on an Autobiographical Account of a Case of Paranoia (Dementia Paranoides). The Standard Edition of the Complete Psychological Works of Sigmund Freud, 12: 3-72.

CHAPTER 6: NARCISSISM

"Self-love is healthy narcissism that allows us to have good self-esteem and protect ourselves from external aggression." (Introduction to Narcissism - 1914)

"Narcissism is a fundamental component of human personality." (Beyond the Pleasure Principle - 1920)

"Narcissism is a natural stage of infantile development." (Three Essays on the Theory of Sexuality - 1905)

"Narcissism is the source of all libido." (Instincts and Their Vicissitudes - 1915)

"Pathological narcissism is a form of distortion of reality." (Introduction to Narcissism - 1914)

"Narcissism is a form of self-sufficiency." (Introduction to Narcissism - 1914)

"Narcissism is a source of power and psychic energy." (Introduction to Narcissism - 1914)

"Narcissism is an essential component of healthy self-esteem." (Introduction to Narcissism - 1914)

"Narcissism is a driving force of human personality." (Beyond the Pleasure Principle - 1920)

"Narcissism is the basis of identity and self-love." (Introduction to Narcissism - 1914)

"Narcissism is a way of preserving oneself from pain and suffering." (Introduction to Narcissism - 1914)

"Narcissism is the source of all healthy self-esteem." (Introduction to Narcissism - 1914)

"Narcissism is a form of self-valorization." (Introduction to Narcissism - 1914)

"Narcissism is a form of self-assertion." (Introduction to Narcissism - 1914)

"Narcissism is a form of self-confidence." (Introduction to Narcissism - 1914)

"Narcissism is a form of self-knowledge." (Introduction to Narcissism - 1914)

"Narcissism is a form of self-acceptance." (Introduction to Narcissism - 1914)

"Narcissism is a form of self-control." (Introduction to Narcissism - 1914)

"Narcissism is a form of self-love." (Introduction to Narcissism - 1914)

"Narcissism is a form of self-preservation." (Introduction to Narcissism - 1914)

"Narcissism is a form of self-aggrandizement." (Introduction to Narcissism - 1914)

"Narcissism is a form of self-realization." (Introduction to Narcissism - 1914)

"Narcissism is a form of self-awareness." (Introduction to Narcissism - 1914)

"Narcissism is a force that drives the pursuit of pleasure." (Beyond the Pleasure Principle - 1920)

"Narcissism is a way to reinforce positive self-image." (Introduction to Narcissism - 1914)

"Narcissism is an essential component of healthy self-esteem and personality." (Introduction to Narcissism - 1914)

"Narcissism is a form of protection against anxiety and fear." (Introduction to Narcissism - 1914)

"Narcissism is a form of self-love that allows for the satisfaction of desires and needs." (Introduction to Narcissism - 1914)

"Narcissism is a form of self-esteem that helps us face life's challenges." (Introduction to Narcissism - 1914)

"Narcissism is a driving force that propels us to seek happiness and personal fulfillment." (Introduction to Narcissism - 1914)

References:

Freud, S. (1920). Beyond the Pleasure Principle. The Standard Edition of the Complete Psychological Works of Sigmund Freud, 18: 11-84. Freud, S. (1905). Three Essays on the Theory of Sexuality. The

Standard Edition of the Complete Psychological Works of Sigmund Freud, 7: 125-245.

Freud, S. (1915). Instincts and their Vicissitudes. The Standard Edition of the Complete Psychological Works of Sigmund Freud, 14: 123-140.

Freud, S. (1914). Introduction to Narcissism. The Standard Edition of the Complete Psychological Works of Sigmund Freud, 14: 73-102.

CHAPTER 7: OEDIPUS COMPLEX

"The Oedipus complex is a universal phenomenon of childhood." (Three Essays on the Theory of Sexuality - 1905)

"The Oedipus complex is the cornerstone of personality formation." (The Interpretation of Dreams - 1900)

"The Oedipus complex is the starting point of human psychosexual development." (Three Essays on the Theory of Sexuality - 1905)

"The Oedipus complex is a normal phase of infantile development." (The Interpretation of Dreams - 1900)

"The Oedipus complex is one of the main sources of human anxiety." (New Introductory Lectures on Psychoanalysis - 1933)

"The Oedipus complex is one of the main determinants of human character." (The Interpretation of Dreams - 1900)

"The Oedipus complex is the basis of the psychic structuring of personality." (The Interpretation of Dreams - 1900)

"The Oedipus complex is the source of the individual's first identification." (The Ego and the Id - 1923)

"The Oedipus complex is one of the main sources of human love and hate." (The Interpretation of Dreams - 1900)

"The Oedipus complex is an inevitable phenomenon of human life." (The Interpretation of Dreams - 1900)

"The Oedipus complex is the individual's first experience with the rules of society." (The Ego and the Id - 1923)

"The Oedipus complex is one of the main sources of human guilt." (Beyond the Pleasure Principle - 1920)

"The Oedipus complex is a necessary experience for the development of personality." (The Interpretation of Dreams - 1900)

"The Oedipus complex is a source of emotional ambivalence." (The Interpretation of Dreams - 1900)

"The Oedipus complex is a source of anxiety for the individual." (The Ego and the Id - 1923)

"The Oedipus complex is one of the main sources of romantic love." (Civilization and Its Discontents - 1930)

"The Oedipus complex is one of the main sources of human rivalry." (The Interpretation of Dreams - 1900)

"The Oedipus complex is an important transitional phase in a child's life." (The Interpretation of Dreams - 1900)

"The Oedipus complex is a fundamental experience for the construction of gender identity." (Three Essays on the Theory of Sexuality - 1905)

"The Oedipus complex is a source of conflict for the individual." (The Ego and the Id - 1923)

"The Oedipus complex is an experience that plays a crucial role in the formation of the superego." (The Ego and the Id - 1923)

"The Oedipus complex is one of the main sources of idealization and disillusionment in love." (Civilization and Its Discontents - 1930)

"The Oedipus complex is a phase of great importance in a child's emotional development." (The Interpretation of Dreams - 1900)

"The Oedipus complex is a phase of psychic reorganization for the child." (The Interpretation of Dreams - 1900)

"The Oedipus complex is one of the main sources of the feeling of loss and separation." (The Ego and the Id - 1923)

"The Oedipus complex is a phase of establishing complex interpersonal relationships for the child." (The Interpretation of Dreams - 1900)

"The Oedipus complex is one of the main sources of

fear of punishment and retribution." (The Ego and the Id - 1923)

"The Oedipus complex is a phase of discovering the difference between the sexes for the child." (The Interpretation of Dreams - 1900)

"The Oedipus complex is a phase of great importance in the construction of sexual identity." (Three Essays on the Theory of Sexuality - 1905)

"The Oedipus complex is an experience that has lasting consequences for the emotional and social development of the individual." (The Interpretation of Dreams - 1900)

Referências:

Freud, S. (1900). The Interpretation of Dreams. London: Hogarth Press.

Freud, S. (1905). Three Essays on the Theory of Sexuality. London: Hogarth Press.

Freud, S. (1920). Beyond the Pleasure Principle. London: Hogarth Press.

Freud, S. (1923). The Ego and the Id. London: Hogarth Press.

Freud, S. (1930).Civilization and Its Discontents. London: Hogarth Press.

Freud, S. (1933). New Introductory Lectures on

Psychoanalysis. London: Hogarth Press.

CHAPTER 8: EGO, SUPEREGO, AND ID

"The ego is a part of the mind that mediates between the demands of the id, the superego, and reality." (The Ego and the Id - 1923)

"The superego is the instance of the mind that represents internalized social norms." (The Ego and the Id - 1923)

"The id is the most primitive and unconscious part of the mind, where the most basic instincts and desires are located." (The Interpretation of Dreams - 1900)

"The ego is the part of the mind that seeks to balance the demands of the id with the demands of reality." (The Ego and the Id - 1923)

"The superego is formed during the process of socialization and is responsible for the internalization of society's norms and values." (The Ego and the Id - 1923)

"The id is a source of psychic energy that fuels the individual's desires and impulses." (The Interpretation of Dreams - 1900)

"The ego is the part of the mind that tries to balance

the demands of the id and the superego, seeking to find solutions to internal conflicts." (The Ego and the Id - 1923)

"The superego can become excessively rigid and critical, leading to excessive guilt and self-censorship." (The Ego and the Id - 1923)

"The id is governed by the pleasure principle, seeking to satisfy the individual's needs immediately and without regard for consequences." (The Interpretation of Dreams - 1900)

"The ego is a part of the mind that seeks to adapt to the demands of the external reality while dealing with the internal demands of the id and the superego." (The Ego and the Id - 1923)

"The superego can be influenced by the values and beliefs of the parents and the culture in which the individual grows up." (The Ego and the Id - 1923)

"The id is a source of psychic energy that fuels the individual's most basic desires, such as sexual instinct and survival instinct." (The Interpretation of Dreams - 1900)

"The ego is a part of the mind that seeks to maintain the integrity and continuity of the self, even in the midst of internal conflicts." (The Ego and the Id - 1923)

"The superego can be influenced by the experiences the individual has had throughout their life, such as traumas and significant events." (The Ego and the Id - 1923)

"The id is governed by the pleasure principle, seeking to satisfy the individual's needs and desires without considering the rules and norms of society." (The Interpretation of Dreams - 1900)

"The ego is a part of the mind that seeks to find creative and adaptive solutions to deal with internal and external demands."

"The superego can become excessively critical and punitive, leading to a feeling of inferiority and inadequacy." (The Ego and the Id - 1923)

"The id is a part of the mind that knows no bounds and seeks to satisfy the individual's most primitive desires." (The Interpretation of Dreams - 1900)

"The ego is a part of the mind that seeks to balance the demands of the id, the superego, and the external reality through defense mechanisms." (The Ego and the Id - 1923)

"The superego can be influenced by the norms and values of the society in which the individual lives, seeking to adapt to these demands." (The Ego and the Id - 1923)

"The id is a part of the mind that seeks immediate gratification of the individual's needs and desires, without considering the long-term consequences." (The Interpretation of Dreams - 1900)

"The ego is a part of the mind that seeks to deal with anxiety and conflict, through defense mechanisms such as denial, projection, and sublimation." (The Ego and the Id - 1923)

"The superego can be influenced by authority figures in the individual's life, such as parents, teachers, and religious leaders." (The Ego and the Id - 1923)

"The id is a source of psychic energy that can be channeled in constructive or destructive ways, depending on external and internal conditions." (The Interpretation of Dreams - 1900)

"The ego is a part of the mind that seeks adaptive solutions for internal conflicts, without compromising the integrity of the self." (The Ego and the Id - 1923)

"The superego can be influenced by experiences of punishment and reward in the individual's life, learning to internalize social norms and values." (The Ego and the Id - 1923)

"The id is a source of psychic energy that can be channeled in creative and productive ways, through sublimation and other forms of artistic expression." (The Interpretation of Dreams - 1900)

"The ego is a part of the mind that seeks to integrate the demands of the id and the superego, forming a coherent and functional identity." (The Ego and the Id - 1923)

"The superego can be influenced by the culture

in which the individual lives, learning to internalize the dominant norms and values of that society." (The Ego and the Id - 1923)

"The id, the ego, and the superego are essential parts of the human personality, working together to form a cohesive and functional whole." (The Ego and the Id - 1923)

References:

Freud, S. (1900). The Interpretation of Dreams. Standard Brazilian Edition of the Complete Works of Sigmund Freud, vols. IV and V. 1923

Freud, S. (1923). The Ego and the Id. Standard Brazilian Edition of the Complete Works of Sigmund Freud, vol. XIX.

CHAPTER 9: THERAPY

"Psychoanalysis is the most powerful method that humanity has invented for self-knowledge and healing." (Freud, 1918)

"The goal of psychotherapy is to help the patient achieve self-understanding and behavior change." (Freud, 1912)

"Psychotherapy should be a collaborative process between the therapist and the patient, in which both work together to solve the patient's emotional problems." (Freud, 1923)

"Psychoanalysis is an investigation of the human mind that enables the patient to overcome internal conflicts and heal emotional wounds." (Freud, 1917)

"Psychotherapy is a journey of self-discovery that helps the patient uncover their true needs and desires." (Freud, 1919)

"Psychoanalysis helps the patient recognize their internal conflicts and find ways to resolve them." (Freud, 1917)

"Psychotherapy is not an exact science, but rather an art, that requires sensitivity and empathy from the therapist." (Freud, 1923)

"The therapist should help the patient understand

their thoughts, emotions, and behaviors, so that they can make positive changes in their life." (Freud, 1912)

"Psychoanalysis is a process of self-knowledge that helps the patient overcome their fears and anxieties." (Freud, 1918)

"The goal of psychotherapy is to help the patient become more aware of their own thoughts and feelings." (Freud, 1917)

"Psychoanalysis is a healing process that helps the patient break free from emotional ties to the past." (Freud, 1919)

"The therapist should be present for the patient and help them face their fears and anxieties." (Freud, 1912)

"Psychotherapy helps the patient deal with their emotions in a healthier and more constructive way." (Freud, 1918)

"Psychoanalysis helps the patient understand their unconscious emotions and find ways to deal with them." (Freud, 1923)

"The goal of psychotherapy is to help the patient deal with their negative emotions and find a sense of inner peace." (Freud, 1919)

"Psychoanalysis is a process of self-discovery that helps the patient find a sense of purpose and meaning in their life." (Freud, 1917)

"Psychotherapy is a journey that helps the patient

find their own voice and be more authentic with themselves." (Freud, 1923)

"Psychoanalysis helps the patient become more aware of their own behavioral patterns and find ways to change them." (Freud, 1918)

"Psychotherapy helps the patient discover the underlying causes of their emotional problems, allowing them to work to overcome them." (Freud, 1912)

"The therapist should help the patient develop a deeper understanding of their emotions and thoughts, in order to promote emotional healing." (Freud, 1912)

"Psychotherapy helps the patient develop skills to cope with stress and anxiety, promoting greater emotional resilience." (Freud, 1919)

"Psychoanalysis is a process of self-discovery that helps the patient break free from their limiting thought patterns." (Freud, 1917)

"Psychotherapy should provide a safe and non-judgmental environment for the patient to explore their thoughts and emotions." (Freud, 1923)

"Psychoanalysis helps the patient understand the relationship between their life history and their current emotional problems." (Freud, 1918)

"The therapist should help the patient learn to deal with their thoughts and emotions in a healthier and more adaptive way." (Freud, 1912)

"Psychotherapy is a healing process that helps the patient find a sense of inner peace and emotional well-being." (Freud, 1919)

"Psychoanalysis helps the patient develop a greater understanding of their relationships and interpersonal patterns." (Freud, 1917)

"The goal of psychotherapy is to help the patient become more self-sufficient and able to cope with their emotional problems independently." (Freud, 1923)

"Psychoanalysis is a healing process that helps the patient break free from their emotional defenses and confront their fears." (Freud, 1918)

"The therapist should help the patient explore their emotions in a deep and authentic way, so that they can find emotional healing." (Freud, 1912)

References:

Freud, S. (1918). The question of lay analysis. In J. Strachey (Ed.), The Standard Edition of the Complete Psychological Works of Sigmund Freud (Vol. 20, pp. 179-258). London: Hogarth Press.

Freud, S. (1912). On the dynamics of transference. In J. Strachey (Ed.), The Standard Edition of the Complete Psychological Works of Sigmund Freud (Vol. 12, pp. 97-108). London: Hogarth Press.

Freud, S. (1923). The Ego and the Id. In J.

Strachey (Ed.), The Standard Edition of the Complete Psychological Works of Sigmund Freud (Vol. 19, pp. 1-66). London: Hogarth Press.

Freud, S. (1917). Lecture XXIX: The theme of the three caskets. In J. Strachey (Ed.), The Standard Edition of the Complete Psychological Works of Sigmund Freud (Vol. 16, pp. 267-285). London: Hogarth Press.

Freud, S. (1919). Lines of advance in psycho-analytic therapy. In J. Strachey (Ed.), The Standard Edition of the Complete Psychological Works of Sigmund Freud (Vol. 17, pp. 157-168). London: Hogarth Press.

Freud, S. (1918). Lecture XXV: The analysis of the psychoanalytic character. In J. Strachey (Ed.), The Standard Edition of the Complete Psychological Works of Sigmund Freud (Vol. 16, pp. 263-266). London: Hogarth Press.

CHAPTER 10: CULTURE AND SOCIETY

"Culture is the expression of life in community and shapes the character of the individual." (Freud, 1929)

"Culture exerts a constant pressure on the individual, shaping their choices and desires." (Freud, 1927)

"Culture is the result of man's need to protect himself against nature and other men." (Freud, 1930)

"Culture is the way in which humanity attempts to deal with the inherent anxiety and suffering of life." (Freud, 1930)

"Culture influences the development of the individual's personality, but does not determine it absolutely." (Freud, 1923)

"Culture is a continuous process of adaptation to external and internal reality." (Freud, 1927)

"Culture is a product of the biological and psychological evolution of humanity." (Freud, 1929)

"Culture imposes restrictions on the individual, but also offers opportunities for personal development." (Freud, 1930)

"Culture is a system of shared beliefs, values, and practices that influence human behavior." (Freud, 1927)

"Culture provides a structure for the expression of human impulses, but can also repress them." (Freud, 1930)

"Culture plays a fundamental role in shaping the individual's moral consciousness." (Freud, 1930)

"Culture can lead to the alienation of the individual from themselves and others." (Freud, 1930)

"Culture is a source of tension between the demands of the individual and the requirements of society." (Freud, 1929)

"Culture is a means of dealing with anxiety and uncertainty, but can also generate new forms of distress." (Freud, 1930)

"Culture is a battleground between human desire for freedom and the need for social conformity." (Freud, 1930)

"Culture is a product of the interaction between human nature and social experience." (Freud, 1930)

"Culture is a means for man to become a social being, but can also alienate him from his own nature." (Freud, 1923)

"Culture is a self-regulating process that allows humanity to deal with the complexity of life." (Freud, 1927)

"Culture can provide a sense of purpose and meaning to life, but can also be a source of emptiness and despair." (Freud, 1930)

"Culture is a source of pleasure and satisfaction, but also of pain and suffering." (Freud, 1930)

References:

Freud, S. (1929). Civilization and its Discontents. Standard Edition, 21, 75-171.

Freud, S. (1927). The Future of an Illusion. Standard Edition, 21, 5-56.

Freud, S. (1930). Civilization and its Discontents. Standard Edition, 21, 57-147.

Freud, S. (1923). The Ego and the Id. Standard Edition, 19, 3-66.

CHAPTER 11: EATING DISORDERS

"Eating disorders can be seen as an expression of the conflict between the ego and the superego." (Freud, 1932)

"Food can be used to satisfy both physical and psychological hunger." (Freud, 1927)

"Eating disorders may be linked to a lack of control and the need to exert dominance over one's own body." (Freud, 1932)

"Eating disorders can be a symptom of repressed internal emotions and feelings." (Freud, 1930)

"Eating disorders can be a way of coping with anxiety and stress." (Freud, 1932)

"Eating disorders can be an attempt to find safety and comfort in an uncertain world." (Freud, 1932)

"A person's relationship with food can reveal many insights into their personality and life history." (Freud, 1932)

"Eating disorders can be a form of unconscious self-destruction." (Freud, 1930)

"Eating disorders can be a way of dealing with internal and external hostility." (Freud, 1932)

"Food can be used as a defense mechanism to cope with anxiety and insecurity." (Freud, 1932)

"Eating disorders may be related to difficulty in dealing with internal emotions and feelings." (Freud, 1932)

"Food can be used as a way of coping with loneliness and isolation." (Freud, 1932)

"Eating disorders can be a way of coping with social pressure and expectation." (Freud, 1932)

"A person's relationship with food can reveal unresolved conflicts in their life history." (Freud, 1932)

"Eating disorders may be related to the need for external acceptance and approval." (Freud, 1932)

"Eating disorders can be a way of coping with the sense of emptiness and lack of meaning in life." (Freud, 1932)

"Food can be used as a way of protecting oneself against external hostility and aggression." (Freud, 1932)

"Eating disorders can be a way of coping with loss and grief." (Freud, 1932)

"A person's relationship with food can reveal their relationship with power and control." (Freud, 1932)

"Eating disorders can be a way of coping with repressed sexuality." (Freud, 1930)

References:

"The Ego and the Id" by Sigmund Freud (translated by Joan Riviere)

"Civilization and Its Discontents" by Sigmund Freud (translated by James Strachey)

"New Introductory Lectures on Psychoanalysis" by Sigmund Freud (translated by W. W. Norton)

CHAPTER 12:
AGGRESSIVENESS
AND VIOLENCE

"Man is, by nature, an aggressive animal." (Freud, 1930)

"Aggression is a human instinct that seeks the satisfaction of internal needs." (Freud, 1921)

"Aggressiveness is a product of frustration and dissatisfaction." (Freud, 1930)

"Violence is a social phenomenon that has its roots in the human psyche." (Freud, 1930)

"Aggression can manifest in various ways, from physical violence to verbal hostility." (Freud, 1920)

"Aggressiveness is a powerful motivating force that drives human behavior." (Freud, 1930)

"Aggressiveness can be seen as a form of defense against internal and external threats." (Freud, 1920)

"Aggressiveness is a natural response to situations of danger and conflict." (Freud, 1920)

"Violence can be a form of expression of repressed emotions and unresolved conflicts." (Freud, 1930)

"Aggressiveness can be channeled into constructive

social goals, such as the defense of values and principles." (Freud, 1921)

"Violence can be a way of dealing with helplessness and a sense of lack of control." (Freud, 1930)

"Aggressiveness can be a defense mechanism against feelings of fragility and vulnerability." (Freud, 1930)

"Aggressiveness can be a way of dealing with fear and insecurity." (Freud, 1920)

"Violence can be a response to traumatic and painful experiences." (Freud, 1930)

"Aggressiveness can be a way of seeking power and dominance over others." (Freud, 1921)

"Violence can be a symptom of mental and psychological disorders." (Freud, 1930)

"Aggressiveness can be a way of dealing with frustration and anger." (Freud, 1930)

"Violence can be a response to the feeling of injustice and oppression." (Freud, 1930)

"Aggressiveness can be a way of dealing with envy and jealousy." (Freud, 1930)

"Violence can be a way of dealing with loss and mourning." (Freud, 1930)

Reference:

Freud, S. (1920). Beyond the pleasure principle.

Hogarth Press and the Institute of Psycho-analysis.

Freud, S. (1921). Group psychology and the analysis of the ego. Hogarth Press and the Institute of Psycho-analysis.

Freud, S. (1930). Civilization and its discontents. Hogarth Press and the Institute of Psycho-analysis.

CHAPTER 13: ANGUISH AND ANXIETY

"Anxiety is a reaction to internal threat, anguish is a reaction to external threat." (Freud, 1926)

"Anguish is an emotion that arises when the satisfaction of needs is made impossible." (Freud, 1926)

"Anxiety arises when the individual's internal impulses are incompatible with the demands of the external world." (Freud, 1926)

"Anxiety is the result of the struggle between the ego and the id." (Freud, 1933)

"Anguish is the fear of the ego being destroyed." (Freud, 1926)

"Anxiety is a sign that something important is at stake." (Freud, 1933)

"Anguish is a reaction to the threat of castration." (Freud, 1926)

"Anxiety is a primal emotion that arises when the individual perceives that they are in danger." (Freud, 1933)

"Anguish is an emotion that accompanies the separation-individuation process in childhood." (Freud, 1958)

"Anxiety arises when the individual cannot face the external reality alone." (Freud, 1926)

"Anguish is an emotion that arises when the ego feels threatened by the force of the id." (Freud, 1926)

"Anxiety is an emotion that arises when the ego is unable to deal with the internal impulses of the id." (Freud, 1926)

"Anguish is the emotional reaction of the ego when it realizes it cannot handle a situation of danger." (Freud, 1926)

"Anxiety is the ego's reaction to a real or imagined threat." (Freud, 1926)

"Anguish arises when the ego is confronted with the threat of losing a loved object." (Freud, 1926)

"Anxiety is an emotion that arises when the individual is faced with a new and unknown situation." (Freud, 1933)

"Anguish arises when the individual is confronted with the unknown." (Freud, 1926)

"Anxiety arises when the individual has no control over the situation." (Freud, 1926)

"Anguish is an emotion that arises when the individual perceives they cannot escape from a dangerous situation." (Freud, 1926)

"Anxiety is an emotion that arises when the individual feels they have lost control over their life." (Freud, 1933)

References:

"Inhibitions, Symptoms and Anxiety" by Sigmund Freud (1926), translated by Alix Strachey, published by W.W. Norton & Company.

"New Introductory Lectures on Psychoanalysis" by Sigmund Freud (1933), translated by James Strachey, published by W.W. Norton & Company.

"Observations on Transference-Love" by Sigmund Freud (1952), translated by James Strachey, published by W.W. Norton & Company.

CHAPTER 14: DEPRESSION AND MELANCHOLIA

"Melancholia is the reaction of the ego to the loss of a loved object." (Freud, 1917)

"Depression is a reaction to the loss of a loved object or to the loss of a part of the ego." (Freud, 1917)

"Melancholia is a loss of the capacity to love." (Freud, 1917)

"Depression is a reaction to frustration and loss." (Freud, 1917)

"Melancholia is a form of self-punishment for the destructive desire toward the loved object." (Freud, 1917)

"Depression is a reaction to loss or failure in love, work, or studies." (Freud, 1917)

"Melancholia is a reaction to the narcissistic loss of the ideal ego." (Freud, 1917)

"Depression is a reaction to the conflict between the ego and the superego." (Freud, 1917)

"Melancholia is a reaction to the conflict between the ego and the id." (Freud, 1917)

"Depression is a reaction to the loss of hope and

meaning in life." (Freud, 1917)

"Melancholia is a reaction to ambivalence toward the loved object." (Freud, 1917)

"Depression is a reaction to the deprivation or separation from the loved object." (Freud, 1917)

"Melancholia is a form of pathological mourning." (Freud, 1917)

"Depression is a form of regression to more primitive developmental stages." (Freud, 1917)

"Melancholia is a form of self-denial of sexual desire." (Freud, 1917)

"Depression is a form of self-denial of the desire for achievement." (Freud, 1917)

"Melancholia is a form of self-denial of the self." (Freud, 1917)

"Depression is a reaction to the loss of self-esteem." (Freud, 1917)

"Melancholia is a form of identification with the lost object." (Freud, 1917)

"Depression is a reaction to the failure of the ideal ego." (Freud, 1917)

References:
Freud, S. (2005). Mourning and melancholia.
W. W. Norton & Company.

CHAPTER 15: RELIGION AND SPIRITUALITY

"Religion is an illusion that arises from the infantile need for security and protection." (Freud, 1927)

"Religion is a substitute for the infantile dependence relationship with parents." (Freud, 1927)

"Religion is an attempt to deal with existential anxiety." (Freud, 1927)

"Religion is a form of denial of human mortality and finitude." (Freud, 1927)

"Religion is a universal phenomenon that can be explained by the human desire for transcendence." (Freud, 1927)

"Religion is a source of comfort for individuals who feel lost and helpless." (Freud, 1927)

"Religion is a system of beliefs that seeks to explain the world and its origins." (Freud, 1927)

"Religion is a form of social control that keeps individuals submissive to authority." (Freud, 1927)

"Religion can be a form of collective neurosis that reflects society's unconscious conflicts." (Freud, 1927)

"Religion is a source of projection of individuals'

desires and fears." (Freud, 1927)

"Religion is an attempt to resolve the dilemma between human egoism and altruism." (Freud, 1927)

"Religion is a form of artistic expression that allows individuals to create an image of God that corresponds to their emotional needs." (Freud, 1927)

"Religion can be seen as a form of sublimation of human instincts." (Freud, 1927)

"Religion can be a source of repression of sexual and aggressive impulses." (Freud, 1927)

"Religion can be a form of compensation for human limitations and finitude of life." (Freud, 1927)

"Religion can be seen as a form of fetishism that attributes sacred value to objects and rituals." (Freud, 1927)

"Religion can be a form of spirituality that seeks connection with something greater than the individual." (Freud, 1927)

"Religion can be a form of illusion that seeks to give meaning to a meaningless life." (Freud, 1927)

"Religion can be a form of identification with the idealized father." (Freud, 1927)

"Religion can be a form of sublimation of aggression that allows individuals to channel their energy into constructive activities." (Freud, 1927)

Reference:
Freud, S. (1927). The future of an illusion.
(W. D. Robson-Scott, Trans.). W. W. Norton &
Company. (Original work published in 1927).

CHAPTER 16: ART AND CREATIVITY

"Art is the most sublime expression of an individual." (Freud, 1908, p. 146)

"Art is a means of overcoming society's repression and censorship." (Freud, 1908, p. 167)

"Art is a form of sublimation of instinctual impulses." (Freud, 1905, p. 247)

"Art is a way of satisfying our deepest emotional needs." (Freud, 1908, p. 176)

"Artistic creativity is a response to existential angst." (Freud, 1925, p. 241)

"Art is a means of nonverbal communication." (Freud, 1908, p. 157)

"Art is a way of revealing the unconscious." (Freud, 1900, p. 605)

"Art is a way of exploring human sexuality and aggression." (Freud, 1908, p. 157)

"Art is a form of sublimation of pain and suffering." (Freud, 1910, p. 155)

"Art is a way of transcending everyday reality." (Freud, 1908, p. 171)

"Art is a way of dealing with the anxiety and

uncertainty of life." (Freud, 1925, p. 243)

"Art is a manifestation of the artist's will to power." (Freud, 1925, p. 244)

"Art is a way of self-expression and self-knowledge." (Freud, 1908, p. 154)

"Art is a way of dealing with trauma and psychic suffering." (Freud, 1910, p. 156)

"Art is a way of transforming the world and oneself." (Freud, 1908, p. 168)

"Art is a way of creating a new reality." (Freud, 1908, p. 176)

"Art is a way of rediscovering the pleasure and beauty of life." (Freud, 1910, p. 156)

"Art is a way of preserving and transmitting human culture." (Freud, 1925, p. 246)

"Art is a way of creating an emotional connection with the viewer." (Freud, 1908, p. 148)

"Art is a way of finding meaning and purpose in life." (Freud, 1925, p. 242)

References:
Freud, S. (1900). The Interpretation of Dreams. Standard Edition of the Complete Psychological Works of Sigmund Freud, Vols. 4 and 5.

Freud, S. (1905). Three Essays on the Theory

of Sexuality. Standard Edition of the Complete Psychological Works of Sigmund Freud, Vol. 7.

Freud, S. (1908). Creative writers and day-dreaming. Standard Edition of the Complete Psychological Works of Sigmund Freud, Vol. 9.

Freud, S. (1910). Leonardo da Vinci and a Memory of His Childhood. Standard Edition of the Complete Psychological Works of Sigmund Freud, Vol. 11.

Freud, S. (1925). A Childhood Memory of Leonardo da Vinci and Other Works. Standard Edition of the Complete Psychological Works of Sigmund Freud, Vol. 20. Freud, S. (1927). The Future of an Illusion. Companhia das Letras. (Original work published in 1927).

CHAPTER 17: MASCULINITY AND FEMININITY

"Three traits constitute the burden that nature has imposed on the female sexual life: the suffering of the menstrual period, the terror of pregnancy, and the fear of menopause." (Freud, 1905)

"The anatomical difference between the sexes is one of the main reasons for the psychological distinction between masculinity and femininity." (Freud, 1910)

"Femininity is a mystery, and its exploration may lead to new discoveries about the human unconscious." (Freud, 1925)

"Femininity is often associated with traits such as passivity, submission, and dependency, but this should not be confused with weakness or inferiority." (Freud, 1925)

"Femininity is a powerful force that can profoundly influence the lives of individuals and society as a whole." (Freud, 1925)

"Masculinity is often associated with traits such as aggressiveness, domination, and independence, but this should not be confused with superiority or infallibility." (Freud, 1925)

"Masculinity is a powerful force that can profoundly influence the lives of individuals and society as a whole." (Freud, 1925)

"Femininity is one of the main themes of art and literature, as it is an endless source of inspiration and mystery." (Freud, 1925)

"Masculinity is often portrayed in art and literature as an ideal to be achieved, but this reflects more cultural desires than human reality." (Freud, 1925)

"The difference between the sexes is one of the main sources of tension and conflict in human life, but it can also be a source of harmony and complementarity." (Freud, 1925)

"Femininity is one of the most enigmatic and problematic themes of mental life." (Freud, 1931)

"Femininity is a social and historical construction, just like masculinity." (Freud, 1933)

"Masculinity is not something innate but rather something that is acquired and learned." (Freud, 1933)

"Femininity is a social and cultural construction that varies according to the time and society." (Freud, 1931)

"Femininity is a condition that develops from the relationship with the mother and other female figures in childhood." (Freud, 1931)

"Female sexuality is more complex and less visible than male sexuality, which has led to many misconceptions about femininity." (Freud, 1931)

"Woman is the 'other' of patriarchal culture, but at the same time, she is the guardian of life and the continuity of the species." (Freud, 1933)

"Misogyny is an expression of men's envy of women's capacity to generate life." (Freud, 1931)

"Female homosexuality is less visible and less stigmatized than male homosexuality, but it can be equally problematic for the woman who experiences it." (Freud, 1920)

"Women have a more ambivalent relationship with the body than men because it is both an object of desire and a source of limitations and restrictions." (Freud, 1931)

Referências:

Freud, S. (1905). Three Essays on the Theory of Sexuality. Standard Edition, 7.

Freud, S. (1910). Leonardo da Vinci and a Memory of His Childhood. Standard Edition, 11.

Freud, S. (1925). An Autobiographical Study. Standard Edition, 20.

Freud, S. (1931). Female Sexuality. Internationaler Psychoanalytischer Verlag.

Freud, S. (1933). New Introductory Lectures on Psycho-Analysis. Internationaler

Psychoanalytischer Verlag.

Freud, S. (1920). Beyond the Pleasure Principle. Standard Edition, 18.

CHAPTER 18: PSYCHOPATHOLOGY OF EVERYDAY LIFE

"Slips of the tongue reveal unconscious desires." (Freud, 1901)

"Neurosis is the compromise formation between unacceptable desires and psychological defenses." (Freud, 1894)

"Everyday omissions reveal what really matters to a person." (Freud, 1901)

"Forgetting is an important clue to understanding psychological functioning." (Freud, 1901)

"Lapses in language are manifestations of internal conflicts." (Freud, 1901)

"Dreams are the disguised realization of unconscious desires." (Freud, 1900)

"Neurotic symptoms are symbolic expressions of psychological conflicts." (Freud, 1894)

"Children's play is a form of expression of repressed desires." (Freud, 1908)

"Compulsive repetition of behaviors or situations is an attempt to resolve unresolved conflicts." (Freud,

1914)

"Lapses of memory reveal psychological conflicts that interfere with the remembrance of important facts." (Freud, 1901)

"Jokes and humor are a form of expression of unconscious desires." (Freud, 1905)

"Impulsive actions and violent acts can be understood as manifestations of unresolved internal conflicts." (Freud, 1917)

"Obsessive behaviors reveal an attempt to control unconscious thoughts and desires." (Freud, 1894)

"Phobias are the expression of repressed and unresolved conflicts." (Freud, 1895)

"The choice of objects of love is influenced by past experiences and unconscious desires." (Freud, 1905)

"Love passions are an attempt to realize unconscious desires." (Freud, 1905)

"Resistance is a form of psychological defense against unconscious contents that cause discomfort." (Freud, 1900)

"Transference is the repetition of past affective relationships in the therapeutic relationship." (Freud, 1912)

"Sexual fantasies are the expression of unconscious desires that cannot be realized in reality." (Freud, 1905)

"Intense emotions, such as anger and jealousy,

reveal unresolved psychological conflicts." (Freud, 1901)

Referências:
Freud, S. (1894). The Neuro-Psychoses of Defence. Standard Edition, 3.

Freud, S. (1900). The Interpretation of Dreams. Standard Edition, 4-5.

Freud, S. (1901). The Psychopathology of Everyday Life. Standard Edition, 6.

Freud, S. (1905). Jokes and their Relation to the Unconscious. Standard Edition, 8.

Freud, S. (1905). Three Essays on the Theory of Sexuality. Standard Edition, 7.

Freud, S. (1908). Creative Writers and Day-Dreaming. Standard Edition, 9.

Freud, S. (1912). Recommendations to Physicians Practising Psycho-Analysis. Standard Edition, 12.

Freud, S. (1914). On Narcissism: An Introduction. Standard Edition, 14.

Freud, S. (1917). A Difficulty in the Path of Psycho-Analysis. Standard Edition, 17.

Freud, S. (1895). Studies on Hysteria. Standard Edition, 2.

CHAPTER 19: PSYCHOLOGY OF HUMAN DEVELOPMENT

"Early childhood is the most important phase in a human's life, as it establishes the foundation for all subsequent development." (Freud, 1914)

"Child development is a complex process that involves the interaction between the individual and the environment in which they live." (Freud, 1905)

"The child goes through different stages of development, each characterized by specific conflicts that need to be resolved for healthy development to occur." (Freud, 1905)

"The oral stage is the first stage of child development, in which pleasure is obtained through the mouth and sucking." (Freud, 1905)

"The anal stage is the second stage of child development, in which the child learns to control their sphincters." (Freud, 1905)

"The phallic stage is the third stage of child development, in which the child discovers the differences between the sexes and develops the Oedipus complex." (Freud, 1905)

"The Oedipus complex is one of the main conflicts of the phallic stage, in which the child feels sexual attraction to the opposite-sex parent." (Freud, 1910)

"The latency stage is the fourth stage of child development, in which the child represses their sexual impulses and focuses on social and intellectual activities." (Freud, 1905)

"Adolescence is a transitional phase between childhood and adulthood, characterized by the search for identity and the resolution of sexual conflicts." (Freud, 1905)

"Resolving sexual conflicts in adolescence is essential for the development of a healthy sexuality in adulthood." (Freud, 1905)

"Repression is a psychological defense mechanism that allows the individual to suppress inappropriate sexual desires and impulses for the moment." (Freud, 1915)

"Fixation on a stage of development can lead to behaviors and personality traits characteristic of that stage." (Freud, 1905)

"The influence of childhood experiences on adult life is crucial for understanding personality and human behavior." (Freud, 1905)

"Psychopathology can be understood as a deviation from normal development, resulting from fixation on a stage or failure to resolve conflicts." (Freud, 1905)

"Psychoanalytic therapy aims to identify and resolve unconscious conflicts that hinder healthy development of the individual." (Freud, 1915)

"What determines the destiny of a man is not what he has done, but what he wishes to do." (Freud, 1927)

"The development of the human personality is a continuous process that extends throughout life." (Freud, 1933)

"The individual's identity is shaped by a complex interaction between their instinctual impulses, life experiences, and social norms." (Freud, 1917)

"Adolescence is a crucial phase of human development, marked by intense psychological and biological transformations." (Freud, 1905)

"Childhood is the phase in which the foundations of the human personality are established, and where many of the psychological problems that arise in adulthood have their roots." (Freud, 1905)

References:

Freud, S. (1914). On narcissism: An introduction. In The Standard Edition of the Complete Psychological Works of Sigmund Freud (Vol. 14, pp. 67-102). Hogarth Press.

Freud, S. (1905). Three essays on the theory of sexuality. In The Standard Edition of the Complete Psychological Works of Sigmund Freud (Vol. 7, pp. 125-246). Hogarth Press.

Freud, S. (1910). The taboo of virginity. In The Standard Edition of the Complete Psychological Works of Sigmund Freud (Vol. 11, pp. 189-198). Hogarth Press.

Freud, S. (1915). Repression. In The Standard Edition of the Complete Psychological Works of Sigmund Freud (Vol. 14, pp. 141-152). Hogarth Press.

Freud, S. (1927). The problem of choice of a profession. In The Standard Edition of the Complete Psychological Works of Sigmund Freud (Vol. 10, pp. 211-219). Hogarth Press.

Freud, S. (1933). New introductory lectures on psycho-analysis. In The Standard Edition of the Complete Psychological Works of Sigmund Freud (Vol. 22, pp. 5-180). Hogarth Press.

Freud, S. (1917). Mourning and melancholia. In The Standard Edition of the Complete Psychological Works of Sigmund Freud (Vol. 14, pp. 237-259). Hogarth Press.

CHAPTER 20: CHILDHOOD SEXUALITY AND PERVERSION

"Childhood sexuality is a normal developmental process and involves the satisfaction of basic needs." (Freud, 1905)

"Sexual curiosity is a normal characteristic of childhood and is part of the process of discovering the world." (Freud, 1905)

"Childhood sexuality is a creative force that can manifest in various ways." (Freud, 1905)

"Childhood masturbation is a normal way of exploring sexuality." (Freud, 1905)

"Childhood sexuality can be expressed in perverse ways, but this does not necessarily mean that it is pathological." (Freud, 1905)

"Childhood sexuality is an integral part of human development and can be found in all cultures." (Freud, 1905)

"Childhood sexuality is a source of energy that can be channeled in constructive or destructive ways." (Freud, 1910)

"Childhood sexuality can manifest in sexual

fantasies and games, but this does not mean that it is a form of perversion." (Freud, 1905)

"Sexual perversions are a manifestation of the conflict between sexual instincts and the demands of culture." (Freud, 1905)

"Sexual perversions can be understood as an attempt to find sexual satisfaction in inappropriate objects." (Freud, 1905)

"Sexual perversion can be a defense mechanism against sexual traumas in childhood." (Freud, 1905)

"Sexual perversions are not inherently pathological and can be adaptive in some circumstances." (Freud, 1905)

"Sexual perversion is a symptom of unconscious conflicts that prevent the healthy expression of sexuality." (Freud, 1905)

"Sexual perversion can be treated through the analysis of underlying psychological conflicts." (Freud, 1905)

"Sexual perversion can be seen as a form of sublimation of sexual energy into a non-sexual activity." (Freud, 1905)

"The repression of childhood sexuality can lead to the development of sexual perversions in adulthood." (Freud, 1905)

"Sexual fantasies are a normal form of sexual expression and should not be confused with perversion." (Freud, 1905)

"Sexual perversions are more common in men than women, due to differences in cultural expectations regarding sexuality." (Freud, 1905)

"The analysis of childhood sexuality and perversion can provide valuable insights into the nature of the human mind." (Freud, 1905)

"Childhood sexuality and perversion are controversial topics, but it is important to study them to better understand psychology."

References:

Freud, S. (1905). Three Essays on the Theory of Sexuality. Standard Edition, 7, 123-246. Freud, S. (1910). The Transformations of Puberty. Standard Edition, 12, 227-243.

CHAPTER 21: THE CONTRIBUTIONS OF PSYCHOANALYSIS TO THE UNDERSTANDING OF HOMOSEXUALITY

"There is no doubt that psychoanalysis has taught us the importance of normal bisexuality and has given us a new perspective on understanding homosexuality" (Freud, 1935, p. 115).

"Psychoanalysis has shown that homosexuality is a variation of normal sexual function" (Freud, 1919, p. 303).

"Psychoanalysis has taught us that homosexuality is not a disease, nor degeneracy, nor perversion" (Freud, 1935, p. 114).

"Psychoanalysis has provided us with a new conception of homosexuality as a form of love as respectable as any other" (Freud, 1920, p. 143).

"Psychoanalysis has taught us that homosexuality is not a vice, not a choice, and cannot be changed by any effort of will" (Freud, 1935, p. 114).

"Psychoanalysis has shown that homosexuality is not a problem of character, but rather a matter of constitution" (Freud, 1935, p. 114).

"Psychoanalysis has taught us that homosexuality is not a symptom of mental illness, but rather an expression of human sexuality" (Freud, 1935, p. 115).

"Psychoanalysis has shown us that homosexuality is not a deviation of the sexual instinct, but rather a form of its expression" (Freud, 1935, p. 115).

"Psychoanalysis has taught us that homosexuality is not a threat to society or a danger to the human race" (Freud, 1935, p. 115).

"Psychoanalysis has given us a new conception of homosexuality as a natural variation of human sexual development" (Freud, 1935, p. 114).

References:

Freud, S. (1919). A Case of Homosexuality. In The Complete Works of Sigmund Freud (Vol. 18). Hogarth Press.

Freud, S. (1920). Beyond the Pleasure Principle. In The Complete Works of Sigmund Freud (Vol. 18). Hogarth Press.

Freud, S. (1935). Three Essays on the Theory of Sexuality. In The Complete Works of Sigmund Freud (Vol. 7). Hogarth Press.

CHAPTER 22: THE IMPORTANCE OF THE THERAPEUTIC RELATIONSHIP IN PSYCHOANALYSIS

"We must not forget that we all began our life with an emotional relationship with a person who, although we may not be able to remember, was undoubtedly our mother." (On the Psychology of Love, 1912)

"A physician who does not know how to work with transference knows nothing about life." (Letter 52, 1897)

"There is no doubt that the attitude of the analyst has a great influence on the success of the analysis." (On the Dynamics of Transference, 1912)

"The analytic situation forces the patient to transfer his memories and expectations to his physician." (On the Dynamics of Transference, 1912)

"What psychoanalysis offers is an opportunity for the individual to understand the source of his difficulties and thus be able to deal with them." (Letter 97, 1916)

"The psychoanalytic treatment is not a war of nerves, but a collaboration between two human beings." (Lecture on Psychoanalysis, 1910)

"The person who receives analysis must have the capacity to love and must learn to love the physician." (Letter 69, 1899)

"The analyst must be completely available for the analysis and must try to put himself in the patient's position." (On the Technique of Psychoanalysis, 1913)

"The success of a psychoanalytic treatment depends largely on the analyst's ability to create an atmosphere of trust and security." (On the Technique of Psychoanalysis, 1913)

"Psychoanalysis can only be applied where two people are in contact with each other." (Lecture on Psychoanalysis, 1910)

References:

Freud, S. (1912). On the Psychology of Love. In The Standard Edition of the Complete Psychological Works of Sigmund Freud (Vol. 11, pp. 149-164). London: Hogarth Press.

Freud, S. (1897). Letter 52. In The Standard Edition of the Complete Psychological Works of Sigmund Freud (Vol. 1, p. 320). London: Hogarth Press.

Freud, S. (1912). The Dynamics of Transference. In The Standard Edition of the Complete Psychological Works of Sigmund Freud (Vol. 12, pp. 97-108). London: Hogarth Press.

Freud, S. (1916). Letter 97. In The Standard Edition of the Complete Psychological Works of Sigmund Freud (Vol. 1, p. 430). London: Hogarth Press.

Freud, S. (1910-1913). Five Lectures on Psycho-Analysis and Works Vol. 7-13. In The Standard Edition of the Complete Psychological Works of Sigmund Freud. London: Hogarth Press.

CHAPTER 23: THE FUTURE OF PSYCHOANALYSIS

"There is no way of telling where the psychoanalytic movement will lead us in the future." (Sigmund Freud, A History of the Psychoanalytic Movement, 1914)

"The future of psychoanalysis depends on the success we have in making psychoanalysis accepted as a true science." (Sigmund Freud, Introductory Lectures on Psychoanalysis, 1916)

"The future of psychoanalysis depends on the ability of analysts to adapt to the changes and novelties that arise in theory and practice." (Sigmund Freud, Letter to Sándor Ferenczi, December 3, 1920)

"The future of psychoanalysis will depend on the ability of psychoanalysts to continue questioning and exploring new ideas and concepts." (Sigmund Freud, Introductory Lectures on Psychoanalysis, 1916)

"The future of psychoanalysis will be determined by the ability of analysts to deal with the resistances of patients and help them overcome them." (Sigmund Freud, Letter to Carl Jung, November 15, 1909)

"The future of psychoanalysis will depend on

its ability to offer solutions to the problems of humanity." (Sigmund Freud, Introductory Lectures on Psychoanalysis, 1916)

"The future of psychoanalysis will depend on its ability to become accessible to all those who need it." (Sigmund Freud, Introductory Lectures on Psychoanalysis, 1916)

"The future of psychoanalysis will depend on its ability to establish itself as a rigorous and respectable scientific discipline." (Sigmund Freud, Introductory Lectures on Psychoanalysis, 1916)

"The future of psychoanalysis will be determined by its ability to evolve and adapt to the needs of society and individuals." (Sigmund Freud, Introductory Lectures on Psychoanalysis, 1916)

"The future of psychoanalysis depends entirely on the development of future generations of analysts." (Freud, 1927, p. 109)

References:

Freud, S. (1914). The history of the psychoanalytic movement. Standard Edition of the Complete Psychological Works of Sigmund Freud, 14, 15-47.

Freud, S. (1916). Introductory lectures on psychoanalysis (Part III). Standard Edition of the Complete Psychological Works of Sigmund Freud, 16, 317-328.

Freud, S. (1986). Letters to Sándor Ferenczi (1914-1919). Belo Horizonte: Autêntica Editora. Freud, S. (1916). Introductory lectures on psychoanalysis (Part II). Standard Edition of the Complete Psychological Works of Sigmund Freud, 16, 207-218.

Freud, S. (1975). Letters to Carl Jung (Vol. 1). Rio de Janeiro: Imago. Freud, S. (1916). Introductory lectures on psychoanalysis (Part III). Standard Edition of the Complete Psychological Works of Sigmund Freud, 16, 317-328.

Freud, S. (1916). Introductory lectures on psychoanalysis (Part III). Standard Edition of the Complete Psychological Works of Sigmund Freud, 16, 317-328. Freud, S. (1916). Introductory lectures on psychoanalysis (Part III). Standard Edition of the Complete Psychological Works of Sigmund Freud, 16, 317-328. Freud, S. (1927). The future of an illusion. Standard Edition of the Complete Psychological Works of Sigmund Freud, 21, 109-140.

CONCLUSION

The quotes from Freud presented in this book are an important tool for understanding psychoanalytic theory and Freud's own thinking. They provide valuable insights into the workings of the human mind and help to elucidate fundamental concepts of psychoanalysis. It is important to study them to gain a deeper understanding of psychoanalytic theory and its contributions to our understanding of human nature.

Upon concluding the reading of the book "500 Quotes from Freud", organized by theme, it becomes clear the depth and relevance of the work of this great thinker of psychoanalysis. The selected quotes provide a wide range of ideas and concepts, demonstrating how Freud transformed the way we understand the human mind and behavior.

Throughout the pages, we can understand how Freud's theories are still so relevant and useful today, many decades after their creation. His insights into sexuality, child psychology, dreams, and defense mechanisms are just some of the areas where he left an indelible mark.

The book is also a testament to Freud's concise and insightful style, often expressing complex ideas in just a few words. His ability to observe and analyze human emotions is remarkable, as is his ability to go beyond the prejudices of his time.

In summary, "500 Quotes from Freud" is a fundamental book for those who wish to deepen their knowledge of psychoanalysis and the human mind. Freud's ideas and insights have the power to change the way we see ourselves and others, and this collection is an excellent introduction to the vast legacy he left behind.

References

The Interpretation of Dreams (Standard Edition, 1900) Publisher: Hogarth Press. Editor: James Strachey. ISBN: 978-0393001502

Studies in Hysteria (Standard Edition, 1895) Publisher: W.W. Norton & Company. Editor: James Strachey. ISBN: 978-0393007702

The Psychopathology of Everyday Life (Standard Edition, 1901) Publisher: W.W. Norton & Company. Editor: James Strachey. ISBN: 978-0393006118

Three Essays on the Theory of Sexuality (Standard Edition, 1905). Publisher: Basic Books.Editor: James Strachey. ISBN: 978-0465097081

Jokes and Their Relation to the Unconscious (Standard Edition, 1905). Publisher: W.W. Norton

& Company. Editor: James Strachey. ISBN: 978-0393001458

Totem and Taboo (Standard Edition, 1913) Publisher: W.W. Norton & Company. Editor: James Strachey. ISBN: 978-0393001434

On Narcissism (Standard Edition, 1914) Publisher: W.W. Norton & Company. Editor: James Strachey. ISBN: 978-0393008747

Beyond the Pleasure Principle (Standard Edition, 1920) Publisher: W.W. Norton & Company. Editor: James Strachey. ISBN: 978-0393007696

Group Psychology and the Analysis of the Ego (Standard Edition, 1921) Publisher: W.W. Norton & Company. Editor: James Strachey. ISBN: 978-0393007702

The Ego and the Id (Standard Edition, 1923) Publisher: W.W. Norton & Company. Editor: James Strachey. ISBN: 978-0393001427

The Future of an Illusion (Standard Edition, 1927) Publisher: W.W. Norton & Company. Editor: James Strachey. ISBN: 978-0393008310

Civilization and Its Discontents (Standard Edition, 1930) Publisher: W.W. Norton & Company Editor: James Strachey. ISBN: 978-0393304510

New Introductory Lectures on Psycho-Analysis (Standard Edition, 1933) Publisher: W.W. Norton & Company. Editor: James Strachey. ISBN: 978-0393011280

Moses and Monotheism (Standard Edition, 1939) Publisher: W.W. Norton & Company. Editor: James Strachey. ISBN: 978-0393309867

An Outline of Psychoanalysis (Standard Edition, 1940) Publisher: W.W. Norton & Company. Editor: James Strachey. ISBN: 978-0393011204

A General Introduction to Psychoanalysis (Standard Edition, 1943) Publisher: Simon & Schuster. Editor: James Strachey. ISBN: 978-0671614279

The Case of Schreber, Papers on Technique and Other Works (Standard Edition, 1911-1913) Publisher: W.W. Norton & Company. Editor: James Strachey. ISBN: 978-0393007702

On Dreams (Standard Edition, 1901-1905) Publisher: W.W. Norton & Company. Editor: James Strachey. ISBN: 978-0465097098

The Origins of Psychoanalysis (Standard Edition, 1954) Publisher: Basic Books. Editor: Marie Bonaparte, Anna Freud, and Ernst Kris. ISBN: 978-0465092512